I0059874

Your Amazing Itty Bitty: Getting Financially Organized Checklist

15 Key Steps to Organizing Your Financial Life

Knowing what we have and where to find it can be the foundation for making wise financial decisions throughout life.

Additionally, when the unexpected happens, you may end up in the hospital one day for example, having your records:

- organized and able to be found,
- current,
- and accurately reflecting your wishes,

can ensure a shorter, less stressful, and often less costly experience for you and your family.

Ready for more financial peace of mind? Use this book to help compile your financial records.

This is a "MUST READ" book by everyone. Marie does an exceptional job of providing simple essential tools and techniques to get and stay financially organized for a lifetime! Thank you Marie for creating this book, it is a very important contribution.

Valentino Sabuco, CFP®, Executive Director
The Financial Awareness Foundation
A 501(c)(3) Nonprofit Organization Dedicated to Significantly "Improving financial awareness & financial literacy"

Your Amazing Itty Bitty®: Getting Financially Organized Checklist

15 Key Steps to Organizing Your Financial Life

Marie Burns, CFP®
Certified Financial Planner

Published by Itty Bitty® Publishing
A subsidiary of S & P Productions, Inc.

Copyright © 2019 **Marie Burns**

All rights reserved. No part of this book may be
reproduced or transmitted in any form or by any
means, electronic or mechanical, including
photocopying, recording or by any information
storage and retrieval system, without written
permission of the publisher, except for inclusion
of brief quotations in a review.

Printed in the United States of America

Itty Bitty Publishing
311 Main Street, Suite D
El Segundo, CA 90245
(310) 640-8885

ISBN: 978-1-950326-34-1

This book is intended to be informational
only and is not intended to be construed as
tax, financial, or legal advice. Readers should
consult their own advisors who are licensed
in their state of residence and familiar with
their personal situation.

Dedication

This book is dedicated to those who invest the time and energy into organizing and summarizing their financial records as a gift to themselves and those they care about.

Stop by our Itty Bitty® website to find interesting information about financial organization.

www.IttyBittyPublishing.com

Or visit **Marie Burns** at

www.**MindMoneyMotion**.com

Table of Contents

Introduction

This Itty Bitty book will help you compile a summary and much of the detail regarding your current financial situation. This will assist you throughout your life to:

- Save you time whether it's paying bills, finding information, or doing taxes
- Keep your documents easily available and findable during an emergency
- Help eliminate missed opportunities
- Avoid penalties and/or missed payments

Additionally, people you care about will absolutely need to know this information if you become incapacitated or after you are gone. This book will provide a guide to:

- The content needed to capture your current financial snapshot in one convenient location.
- Help you think through and prepare so that your wishes are known and implemented as needed.
- Remind you to communicate with advisors and family about this topic.

Step 1
Organizing Your Paperwork

Getting and staying organized will be the
foundation for making wise financial decisions
because an overwhelmed or confused mind does
not usually perform effectively. So use whatever
system works best to organize and meet your
needs and then stick with it.

1. Whatever format you choose to get
    organized (a binder, hanging files, a
    workbook, notebook, electronic files),
    keep your filing current and update it
    annually (around tax time or year-end
    is when you are receiving updated
    statements anyway).
2. Use a pencil if handwriting to make
    changes easily. Leave extra space or
    pages in case you need to add
    information later.
3. Give a copy to someone you trust or
    tell someone where to find it.

Congratulations for providing this gift to
yourself AND those you care about!

Getting Organized

- You may want to compile a master list of where your various records can be found listing each item/category and its location.

- For storing original documents that will potentially be needed in the future, consider a fireproof safe at home or as a backup using a safe deposit box at a bank, though that may be sealed at death or unavailable in an emergency.

- If there are items you carry with you, i.e. credit card, driver's license, insurance card, etc., it is a good practice to make a copy of those items to store in your files as well and update those copies as they are replaced.

- Is there a duplicate set of keys (house, vehicle, etc.)? Where are they? Who else has a set? Is that information documented or easily found somewhere?

Step 2
Personal Information

Provide basic information about yourself as well as any significant others in your life:

1. Full name
2. Date of birth
3. Current address and contact information
4. Social Security number
5. Military details, if applicable
6. Church information, if applicable
7. Employer contact information

For a complete set of free forms to compile your personal financial inventory, visit The Financial Awareness Foundation at www.thefinancialawarenessfoundation.org

A few thoughts about passwords

Eventually, someone else may need to access your accounts when you are not available so keep up-to-date records in a secure place of your login information in whatever format you find most helpful (password booklet, password list, app on phone, file on the computer, etc.).

- Account name
- Website address
- Username
- Password
- Other information: security question/answer, where statements can be found if also in a file, phone number of account provider

Let someone you trust know the location of your password inventory via a note identifying its location in a fireproof safe, safe deposit box or sealed envelope to be opened by your trusted person when needed. This significantly reduces the risk of having your private information get into unwanted hands.

Step 3
Family/Other Information

Document details about immediate family, friends, and/or social groups.

1. Names (parents, siblings, children, friends, social group contacts, etc.)
2. Date of birth
3. Date and cause of death, if deceased
4. Current address and contact information
5. Family medical history
6. Marital status
7. Special notes

Including a copy of a family tree also can be helpful in clarifying relationships.

Special Notes

- If there are special circumstances or helpful things to understand about different people or various situations, a note of explanation can be helpful.
- Perhaps someone is typically only reachable on certain days or times, make a note.
- This may also be a section of the records where you want to include a list of important people to be contacted immediately in the event of your hospitalization or death.

Step 4
Advisors

Contact information of not only those who impact your financial health, but also your physical and spiritual health as well.

1. Attorney (estate planning, business, etc.)
2. Banker (personal, mortgage, business, etc.)
3. Insurance agents (home, auto, life, etc.)
4. Tax advisor
5. Financial advisor
6. Business partner
7. Doctor (family physician, specialist, etc.)
8. Clergy
9. Others

Contact information for Advisors

- Business name and website
- Individual name
- Physical address
- Phone number
- Email address
- Notes about availability, if known

Step 5
Income Sources

Document the details about your income sources:
1. Social Security
2. Pension
3. Military
4. Trust income
5. Earned income from an employer
6. Self-employment income
7. Alimony
8. Royalties
9. Dividend and interest income
10. IRA distributions
11. Other income sources

Don't forget to keep files and stay on top of your "hidden paycheck" too---your employer benefits:
- Understand your benefits and their tax treatment
- Keep your primary and secondary beneficiary selections current
- Fully participate in your retirement plans and use other benefits wisely
- Don't be tempted to overstock your net worth with company stock

Tax returns will show additional data

Even though tax returns show annual income, it is helpful to itemize some detail for each income source in your record book or files:

- Approximate dates or time of year each payment is received
- Typical amount received
- Whether taxes have been withheld
- Survivor percentage, if applicable

Step 6
Expense Details

No one likes the word budget but try to itemize as much of the typical household "outflow" (aka budget) in some format i.e. spreadsheet, monthly calendar, itemized list, etc.

1. Include regular monthly expenses (utilities, phone, auto, etc.)
2. Make note of seasonal or non-monthly costs that get paid out i.e. semi-annual or quarterly insurance payments, property taxes, charitable commitments, etc.
3. Debt details i.e. mortgage, credit cards, auto loans, etc.

Common income/expense mistakes to avoid:

1. Spending more than you make
2. Incurring debt by over-spending
3. Not tracking your income and expenses
4. Impulse spending
5. Not having sufficient cash reserves

Why else does this matter?

- Even if you live in the same household with a spouse or significant other, it is very common that one of you regularly takes care of making sure that certain bills are paid and the other is not as involved. So for that person's sake, or think of the family member or friend who may need to step in and help with things if you are in the hospital for a time or to be the executor at some point, that individual has no idea what is paid, when, or why.

- These details can also be helpful in preventing fraud when someone has an idea of what should be going out of an account for legitimate reasons and be more watchful for items that are not on the expense list.

- If you haven't already gotten into the habit of requesting an annual credit report, please start now. In today's world of fraud and identity theft, reviewing your annual credit report can help you keep on top of any credit card abuse you may not be catching. Visit www.annualcreditreport.com

Step 7
Insurance Inventory

For each category of insurance, make sure the following information is available:

1. Type of insurance
2. Insurance company name
3. Policy number
4. Company contact information
5. Agent name and contact data
6. Ideally, the declaration page (single page summarizing the benefits of each policy) could be kept in a folder with the insurance inventory (and be easily accessible in the full insurance file as well)

Typical types of insurance

It can be helpful to make a list of all insurance types and then either fill in the details of each policy, write "see file" after each policy type or write in "NONE" after each policy type. That way it is clear that no one needs to guess about whether they need to look for a policy if it doesn't exist (life insurance or long-term care insurance, for example).

- Vehicle
- Rental
- Homeowners
- Property
- Earthquake / Flood
- Liability
- Personal Liability Umbrella
- Business
- Medical, dental, vision
- Life
- Disability
- Long term care
- Other

Step 8
Net Worth Statement

Your goal is to summarize in one place the value of everything you own, as well as everything you owe (known as a Net Worth Statement).

1. Check out the Net Worth Statement and Historical Net Worth templates available free from The Financial Awareness Foundation at www.TheFinancialAwarenessFoundation.org

2. Date the Net Worth Statement and list all items or account names (referred to as assets) and their current market values as well as balances owed (debt owed is referred to as a liability on a Net Worth Statement).

Tips for Compiling Your Net Worth Statement

- Make sure the account names listed match the company name shown at the top of the statements they reference. For example, if you have a Roth IRA statement from E-trade, list it on the Net Worth Statement as E-trade Roth IRA followed by your name.

- Specify account ownership type in the account name whenever possible. For example, if you are a couple and have a joint investment account at Fidelity list it as a Joint Fidelity account (or Trust Fidelity account if applicable) on the Net Worth Statement.

- If applicable, you may want to itemize the contents of your safe deposit box at the bank and file that list in your banking file. Unless there are items like jewelry, coins, etc., the safe deposit box items (often mainly documents) aren't often listed on the Net Worth Statement.

- Annually copy year-end statements for financial accounts and loans and keep them with your estate & gift plan documents.

Step 9
Cash and Investments

Your cash and non-retirement accounts list/file, often by account or institution, should include:

1. Owner of the account
2. Type of account
3. Name and address of institution
4. Account number
5. Contact information
6. Approximate balance (dated)
7. Name and address of any beneficiaries
8. Check out dozens of Know Where You Stand forms to itemize accounts, personal property, etc. available from The Financial Awareness Foundation free of charge at www.TheFinancialAwarenessFoundation.org

Typical types of cash and non-retirement accounts

- Checking
- Savings
- Money market
- Certificate of deposit (CD)
- Safe deposit box
- Stock certificates
- Individual bonds
- Individual, joint, TOD (Transfer on Death) or trust taxable investment accounts

Step 10
Retirement Accounts

List or have files for your tax deferred
(retirement) accounts showing:

1. Owner of account
2. Type of account
3. Name and address of institution
4. Account number
5. Contact information
6. Approximate balance (dated)
7. Name and address of any beneficiaries

Typical types of retirement accounts

Because each type of retirement account can
have various tax or distribution rules, it is
important to keep them listed/filed
separately:

- Traditional IRA
- Rollover IRA
- Roth IRA (note the year first established)
- Employer plan (401(k), 403(b), 457, etc.)
- Qualified annuity
- Non-qualified annuity

Step 11
Real Property

Document properties you own and important
details:

1. Ownership (i.e. individual, joint with
   rights of survivorship, trust, etc.)
2. Address of property
3. Approximate current market value
4. Purchase date and price
5. Notes about any additions to the property
   including dates and dollar value

Typical types of property

- Primary residence
- Vacation or second home
- Land
- Rental property
- Farmland
- Business property
- Cemetery plot
- Timeshare

Step 12
Personal Property

List or have in a file the general details about
personal property owned:

1. Name of item
2. Purchase date
3. Purchase amount
4. Approximate current market value
5. A photo or video of household and/or
   valuable items can be very helpful for
   valuation, identification, and distribution
   purposes
6. Note if you are referencing this item in
   your will, trust, or in a Personal Property
   Disposition Letter of Instruction to your
   executor or trustee

Typical personal property items

- Antiques
- Art pieces
- Boat
- Collections
- Guns
- Heirloom items
- Home furnishings
- Intellectual property
- Jewelry
- Pets
- Season tickets
- Vehicles

Step 13
Estate & Gift Plan

In addition to having the actual documents stored in your file, safe, or safe deposit box, it is helpful to list the main people involved and their contact information:

1. Estate planning attorney
2. Executor/personal representative/trustee
3. Financial power of attorney and alternate
4. Health care agent and alternate
5. Beneficiaries named in your plan documents
6. Nonprofits named in your plan documents
7. Download the Estate and Gift Planning Location Sheet from The Financial Awareness Foundation at www.TheFinancialAwarenessFoundation.org
8. You may want to store your final wishes and information in a secure, central personal website. Check out www.Everplans.com as one option.

Typical estate planning documents

- Will
- Trust
- Health Care Power of Attorney
- Living Will, wishes for end-of-life medical care (often included in the Health Care Power of Attorney document)
- Durable (financial) Power of Attorney
- Final Wishes (funeral preferences)
- Disposition of Personal Property Letter of Instruction (a signed and dated list of personal property or sentimental items stating who you want to receive those items; you can write or re-write, sign and date this yourself at any time and store it with the will)
- Ethical Will (legacy notes to your family)

Step 14
Common Mistakes to Avoid

Once you have a clearer understanding of your financial picture, you are better positioned to understand some of life's biggest challenges. So in order to know where you stand, steer clear of these missteps:

1. Not regularly preparing, analyzing and updating a list of what you own and owe (net worth statement)
2. Not understanding what you own or owe
3. Increasing your debt due to overspending
4. Incurring high interest debt, especially debt that cannot be repaid immediately
5. Not keeping the title to your assets current with your estate and gift plans
6. Not keeping your beneficiary designations current
7. Not having a sufficient cash reserve and a back-up line of credit
8. Procrastination

Source: The Financial Awareness Foundation

Some general issues to think about once you're organized:

- Putting money aside for the future. Think about savings for shorter term needs and goals (like a vehicle purchase or home down payment) versus investments for longer term plans (like retirement).

- Saving for the "unexpected events" in life. Money magazine once reported that the average American experiences at least one "unexpected event" every 10 years. And those often involve the need for money, so be sure to have an emergency cash reserve built up (3-6 months of living expenses is a basic rule of thumb).

- Ignoring headlines as it relates to your long-term growth goals. Remember that in general, the media is focused on selling headlines not "boring" advice like the importance of diversification, rebalancing, and beating inflation.

Step 15
Miscellaneous

Once you have your financial house in order, consider the following tips:

1. Use automatic deposits and bank transfers to save time, postage, and missed bills as well as to pay yourself first (i.e. an automatic transfer to savings, a 401(K) contribution, an automatic Roth contribution, etc.).
2. Save time and money by reducing the number of payments you make for insurance premiums (i.e. annually vs monthly or quarterly).
3. To protect yourself from unexpected events, keep 6 -12 months of living expenses built up in a readily accessible cash reserve account.
4. As an additional safety net, establish a line of credit (based on the value of your home or a low interest rate credit card set aside for use only in emergencies) before you need it.

Other resources to check out:

You may prefer to use a fill-in-the-blank format to compile and maintain this information. There are several places you can find inventory templates:

- The Financial Awareness Foundation has compiled over 50 templates to get financially organized, available free of charge, at www.TheFinancialAwarenessFoundation.org
- www.whatifworkbook.com
- A book titled Get it Together by Melanie Cullen with Shae Irving
- A book titled The Household Financial Record Book by Chris T. Clark
- A book titled Your Family Records Organizer by Kiplinger
- A book titled Checklist for My Family by Sally Balch Hurme
- A book titled And Then There Was One by Charlotte Fox.

Keep your financial house in order by annually reviewing and updating your checklists and your financial, estate and gift plans.

Having better personal finance knowledge changes your world and the world around you…
FOREVER!

You've finished. Before you go...

Tweet/share that you finished this book.

Please star rate this book.

Reviews are solid gold to writers. Please take a few minutes to give us some itty bitty feedback.

ABOUT THE AUTHOR

Marie Burns started her career helping people balance their diet and exercise as a Registered Dietitian. A dozen years later, she began her journey as a Certified Financial Planner™ Professional and has been helping people balance their finances for almost two decades. Both roles involve guiding others to make behavior changes.

As the oldest of four children as well as the mother of four children, she is a natural fit for serving others as their "financial mother." Coming into the financial industry as a second career has helped Marie avoid the lingo of finance-speak and instead focus on translating complex subjects into understandable English.

When Marie realized that she was getting questions DAILY from friends, clients, and family related to helping aging parents, settling family estates, and couples worrying about how things will go when one of them is no longer around, she knew she needed to write a financial checklist.

Marie's goal is to create The Ripple Effect: these financial checklist books act like a rock launched into a pond and its ripples reach many more lives than she could ever positively impact in person. Marie writes and speaks to groups at www.MindMoneyMotion.com. She advises clients at www.FocusPointPlanning.com.

If you benefitted from this Amazing Itty Bitty® Book, you might also enjoy...

- **Your Amazing Itty Bitty® Eldercare Book** – John Smith RN

- **Your Amazing Itty Bitty® Alzheimers Book** – Dung Trinh, MD

- **Your Amazing Itty Bitty® Financial Checklist Trilogy** (three Itty Bitty Checklist Books in one) – Marie Burns – coming soon

or many of the other Itty Bitty® Books available on line.

www.ingramcontent.com/pod-product-compliance
Lightning Source LLC
Chambersburg PA
CBHW071421200326
41520CB00014B/3527